I0571048

I Spy Vegetables
** 32-Page Condensed Edition **

Other titles by this author:

- *Espío Vegetales: Una Experiencia de Buscar y Encontrar en las Ciencias y las Matemáticas Tempranas* | Spanish w/ English Translation
- *I Spy Fruit: A Seek and Find Early Science and Math Experience* | English
- *Espío Frutas: Una Experiencia de Buscar y Encontrar en las Ciencias y las Matemáticas Tempranas* | Spanish w/ English Translation
- *Fruits and Veggies Row by Row: Children Explain How Plants Grow in Their Garden* | English
- *Frutas y Vegetales Fila por Fila: Los Niños Explican Cómo Crecen las Plantas en su Jardín* | Spanish with English Translation
- *We Eat Food That's Fresh: A Children's Picture Book About Tasting New Foods* (downloadable companion song) | English
- *Comemos Comida Fresca: Un Libro Para Niños Sobre Probando Comidas Nuevas* | Spanish with English Translation
- *Fruits & Veggies Making Faces: A Children's Picture Book About Feelings, Emotions, and Self-Expression (2nd Edition)* | English
- *We Love the Company: A Book About Table Manners* | English
- *Nos Encanta la Compañía: Una Historia Sobre Modales en la Mesa* | Spanish with English Translation
- *When You Find Colors and Shapes : A Physically Interactive Early STEM-Based Children's Picture Book* | English
- *Cuando Encuentres los Colores y las Formas* | Spanish with English Translation
- *Quand Vous Trouvez les Couleurs et les Formes* | French with English Translation

About the Author:

Angela Russ-Ayon resides in Long Beach, California, with her family. She is an author, keynote speaker, producer, and trainer on the subject of early childhood development, as well as the owner of Russ InVision Company children's record label and publishing house. Her company boasts over 1.5 million in sales, has been presented nine early childhood music awards of excellence, and is represented by school suppliers nationwide. Her specialty is engaging young children in interactive music and movement using fine and gross motor activities that get children out of their seats, promote imaginative play, help build brain pathways, and bridge educational gaps.

2nd edition
©2020 Russ InVision Company. All rights reserved.
For information about author visits or permission to reproduce selections of this book, contact:

Russ InVision Company
Long Beach, CA 90808   •   E-mail: info@abridgeclub.com   •   www.AbridgeClub.com

ISBN: 978-1-958627-15-0

IngramSpark Paperback | 32-Page Condensed Edition | Ultra Premium Interior

I spy vegetables.

I spy vegetables that are clean
and vegetables that are dirty.

I spy vegetables that are short.

I spy vegetables that are long.

I spy vegetables that are small
and vegetables that are large.

I spy vegetables that are thin and vegetables that are wide.

I spy vegetables that appear to be heavy and vegetables that appear to be light.

I spy vegetables that are smooth
and vegetables that are lumpy.

I spy vegetables in the basket
and vegetables out of the basket.

I spy vegetables on the top
and vegetables on the bottom.

RED CABBAGE

I spy vegetables in the center.

I spy vegetables close together and vegetables far apart.

I spy vegetables that are chopped into small pieces.

I spy vegetables that are shredded.

I spy vegetables sliced in circles.

I spy vegetables cut in sticks.

I spy vegetables that are peeled.

I spy vegetable seeds.

I spy vegetable bulbs.

I spy vegetable roots.

I spy vegetables in open pods.

I spy vegetable sprouts.

I spy vegetable stems.

I spy a vegetable with a husk.

I spy a vegetable flower.

I spy leafy vegetables.

I spy a vegetable that is cut in half.

I spy vegetables that are whole.

I spy vegetables I can drink.

I spy vegetables that are cooked.

I spy fresh vegetables
that I am ready to eat.

www.ingramcontent.com/pod-product-compliance
Lightning Source LLC
Chambersburg PA
CBRC090841120626
46551CB00008B/716